D1247214

Why'd They Do That?
Strange Customs of the Past

BODY SNATCHING

Gareth Stevens
Publishing

Alix Wood

Please visit our website, **www.garethstevens.com**. For a free color catalog of all our high-quality books, call toll free 1-800-542-2595 or fax 1-877-542-2596

Library of Congress Cataloging-in-Publication Data

Wood, Alix.
Body snatching / by Alix Wood.
  p. cm. -- (Why'd they do that? strange customs of the past)
Includes index.
ISBN 978-1-4339-9573-6 (pbk.)
ISBN 978-1-4339-9574-3 (6-pack)
ISBN 978-1-4339-9572-9 (library binding)
1. Body snatching—Juvenile literature. 2. Grave robbing—Juvenile literature. I. Wood, Alix.
II. Title.
GT3353.W66 2014
364.15—dc23

First Edition

Published in 2014 by
Gareth Stevens Publishing
111 East 14th Street, Suite 349
New York, NY 10003

© Alix Wood Books

Produced for Gareth Stevens by Alix Wood Books
Designed and illustrated by Alix Wood
Picture and content research: Kevin Wood
Editor: Eloise Macgregor
Consultant: Rupert Matthews, the History Man

Photo credits:
Cover, 1, 3 4, 5, 6, 8 top, 9, 10, 11, 15 bottom, 21, 24, 29 © Shutterstock; 8 bottom © Neftali/Shutterstock; 14 top and bottom, 15 top, 22 bottom, 23 top © Kim Traynor; 16 © The White House Historical Association; 17, 20 top © Public Domain; 22 top © University of Aberdeen; 22 middle © Judy Willson; 23 middle © Martyn Gorman; 25 top © Sherurcij; 25 bottom © Walters Art Museum; 28 © Public Domain

Printed in the United States of America

CPSIA compliance information: Batch #CS13GS: For further information contact Gareth Stevens, New York, New York at 1-800-542-2595.-

Contents

Why Body Snatch?

Body snatching is secretly digging up corpses from graveyards. People have practiced body snatching all around the world. Why would anyone want to do that? There were several reasons why dead bodies could be valuable back in the 1800s when body snatching was at its height. Dead bodies are even more useful now than they were back then, too.

The main reason for body snatching in the 1700s and 1800s was to provide medical schools with bodies so students could learn **anatomy**. In Britain, before the Anatomy Act of 1832, the only legal supply of corpses were those of criminals condemned to death and **dissection** by the courts. This did not provide enough subjects for the medical schools and private anatomical schools. During the 1700s many were executed for trivial crimes, but by the 1800s only about 55 people were being sentenced to death each year. Surgeons became desperate for bodies so they could learn their trade.

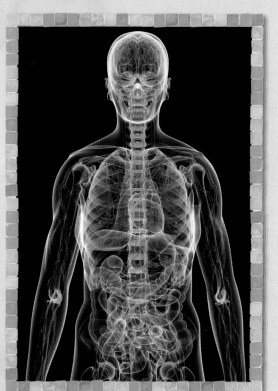

Now we can learn about anatomy from x-rays and imaging cameras, but medical students still practice their skills on donated corpses.

REALLY?

Body snatching was most common in the winter months as the corpses would keep fresh for longer in the cold weather. Anatomy classes usually only ran between October and March for the same reason.

Some artists also employed body snatchers. They wanted corpses to dissect so they could gain an understanding of human anatomy. That knowledge would help them paint or sculpt the human form more accurately.

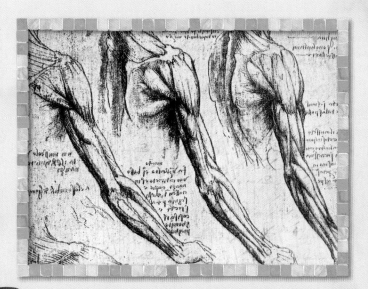

This sketch of a corpse is by the artist Leonardo da Vinci.

WATERLOO TEETH

It wasn't just whole bodies that were snatched. Early false teeth were called "Waterloo teeth." In Europe, in 1815, there was a large battle at Waterloo where many thousands died. At the same time, there was a growing demand for false teeth. People began to scavenge the battlefields for teeth to sell to denture makers!

Surgeons Need Practice

Human dissection has a long history. Greek physicians around 200 BCE dissected human bodies. Before electricity and refrigeration, bodies would quickly decay and become unusable. Body snatching was a good way to supply bodies that were fresh enough to be studied.

By the 1800s, it was common for surgeons to use human corpses for teaching. Doctors would often use the unclaimed bodies of people who had died in their hospitals. When that supply ran out, body snatchers became so indispensible that surgeons would use their influence to keep them out of jail if they were caught. Body snatching was paid well enough to risk being caught, as even without a surgeon's help, the authorities tended to ignore what they considered a necessary evil. Sometimes even the surgeons themselves would turn to body snatching.

REALLY?

In 2006, **archaeologists** digging at one of London's oldest teaching hospitals found the remains of up to 500 people in unmarked graves. The bones were a jumble of skulls with the crowns neatly cut through, bones wired for teaching, or bones clearly dissected. The site is believed to have been a secret burial ground for the adjoining anatomy school.

WILLIAM MILLARD

William Millard was no ordinary body snatcher. He had been the superintendent of anatomy at St Thomas' Hospital, London, under the well-known anatomist and surgeon Astley Cooper. Millard secretly supplied bodies for the surgeon. In 1822, he was fired for selling bodies to Edinburgh and keeping the profit. To support his family, he continued body snatching. He was caught on hospital grounds with a shovel and a sack and sent to Coldbath Prison, where he later died. His wife was angry that her husband was singled out as a grave robber while others got away with it. She published a pamphlet that exposed the network of body snatchers and anatomists, but was sued for **libel** by the editor of the medical journal, *The Lancet*.

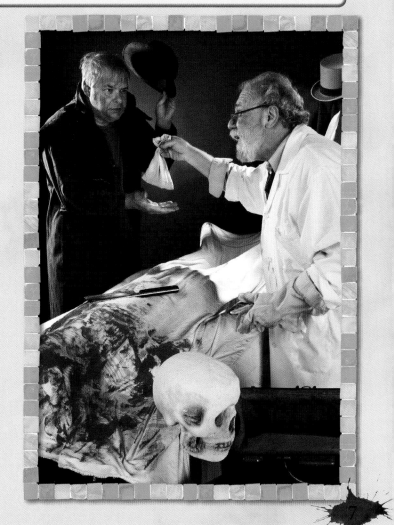

Body-snatcher Thomas Vaughan was employed by surgeon Astley Cooper to supply bodies for his London hospital. Astley Cooper was the son of Vaughan's local vicar in a village northeast of London. He dug up at least 10 bodies from the church graveyard. Before sending the corpses to London, he hid them in sawdust and kept them in houses on the street where he lived. Vaughan was eventually caught and jailed for his crimes.

Artists' Models

LEONARDO DA VINCI

The other professionals that benefitted from an in-depth knowledge of anatomy were artists. It was common for artists such as George Stubbs, famous for painting horses, to dissect and learn the workings of the anatomy of an animal. The same was true of artists that depicted the human form.

Leonardo da Vinci was the painter of the famous portrait, the *Mona Lisa*. He was also an inventor fascinated by machines, and by the most complex machine—the human body. Leonardo believed in drawing straight from life so when drawing the body, he needed a body to study.

The Mona Lisa

In Leonardo's day, dissecting dead bodies was frowned upon and done in secrecy. Leonardo's detailed drawings of the human body were groundbreaking. He sketched the skull from different angles after injecting the brain with hot wax to see all its cavities. He used wires attached to a skeleton's bones to understand human movement. He wrote notes all around the drawings, often written in **mirror-writing** so that other people could not read them. He planned to write a book on anatomy but never finished it.

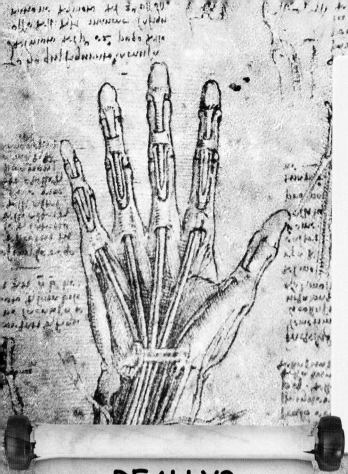

A GRUESOME JOB

Leonardo dissected bodies at night, by candlelight. He held a piece of cloth over his mouth and nose to try and get rid of the smell of the corpses. With the contagious diseases that were around at the time, dissection was very risky for his own health. In his notes, Leonardo warned that the would-be dissectionist "will perhaps be impeded by your stomach... [or] the fear of living through the night hours in the company of quartered and flayed corpses fearful to behold."

REALLY?

In 1514, Leonardo was charged with witchcraft and "necromancy," which means communicating with the dead. His notebooks were analyzed and his drawings of bodies, including a child and a pregnant woman, were considered proof. His left-handed mirror-writing was enough to convict him of witchcraft. His talent just saved him from being put to death!

Leonardo was allowed to dissect criminals, but he is believed to have conducted 30 **autopsies**, and it is unlikely that they were all criminals. He did drawings of a man known as "the centenarian," a toddler, and an unborn child. Leonardo got his bodies from hospitals in Florence, Italy. Sometimes he watched the surgeons there perform operations and autopsies.

How to Steal a Body

A member of a body-snatcher gang would spend the day loitering in a likely graveyard waiting for a funeral. Sometimes they would even join the mourners. When a suitable body was found, two members of the gang would return at night and begin the grisly process of digging up the body.

Body snatching was usually done at night by lamplight. Robbing a grave could take less than an hour. They would dig using a wooden spade, which made the least noise. The earth was moved from the head end of the coffin. The coffin lid was then forced open, and the body was dragged out by the head, often using ropes to pull it. The earth would be replaced so no sign of the theft was apparent. A particular target for body snatchers—also called **resurrectionists** because they made bodies rise from the dead—were the mass graves that the poor were often buried in. These graves were left uncovered until they were full of coffins, so they were an easy target.

BODY-SNATCHING WEATHER

Weather had a major effect on grave-robbing activity. If it was extremely cold, the ground could be very hard to dig in. The best weather was rain as it made the ground easier to dig. Cooler weather meant the bodies wouldn't rot as quickly, too.

REALLY?

Any **shrouds** the corpses were buried in were put back in the grave. There was a popular belief that a body could not be owned, so stealing one wasn't a crime. Stealing a shroud was a crime, however, and could be punished!

Rival body-snatcher gangs would quarrel. Gang members would sometimes deliberately leave a rival's graveyard with obvious signs of body snatching. They would lean empty coffins against walls or leave graves unfilled. The public anger aroused by this could make the rival's graveyard unsafe for weeks, putting the gang out of business!

If the grave was being watched over, there was another way to dig up a corpse. They would remove a man-sized square of earth 15 to 20 feet (5 to 6 m) away from the head of the grave and quietly dig a tunnel to the coffin, which would be about 4 feet (1.2 m) down. The end of the coffin would be pulled off, and the corpse pulled up through the tunnel. The earth was then replaced. Any relatives watching the grave may not notice the small, remote disturbance!

watchman

tunnel

Body-Snatching Britain

Britain became a center of the rather gruesome trade of body snatching. You would assume that the bodies were all dead when they were delivered to the surgeons. This was not always the case!

In 1816 a subject delivered to Joshua Brookes' Theatre of Anatomy was still very much alive. When a "corpse" called Robert Morgan was being rolled down the steps to the cellar, he cried out, "I'm alive!" He was taken to the watch house. John Bottomley, a coachman, was charged with having delivered Morgan to Mr. Brookes tied up in a sack. During the hearing, the "corpse" appeared in the same sack he had been delivered in, except someone had cut out some armholes for him!

The evidence caused much amusement, with Morgan bursting into a fit of laughter at one point. Mr. Brookes stated that a coachman had asked him if he wanted a subject from the notorious London Borough Gang. Mr. Brookes agreed to take it, and a coach had delivered a sack. Mr. Brookes had kicked the sack down two cellar steps before the subject called out.

An Evil Vendetta

The London Borough Gang did not like anatomist Joshua Brookes. They once left two putrefying corpses on the anatomist's doorstep. Two women tripped over the remains and their hysterics drew a crowd that would have probably killed Brookes if the police had not intervened.

The London Borough Gang supplied London's biggest anatomical schools, including that of Astley Cooper. Cooper used his influence to keep them out of jail a number of times and paid any imprisoned member's family a pension while he was in jail. In 1816 they organized a strike against one hospital, refusing to supply any corpses until the price was raised. The school bought corpses from other body snatchers. The Borough Gang broke into the dissecting rooms, threatened the students, and mutilated the rival body snatchers' corpses. The police were called, but to avoid publicity the surgeons were forced to bail the gang out of jail.

REALLY?

Selling bodies was such a good money-maker that some people even murdered children to sell to the highest bidder. Englishman John Bishop was tried and convicted of murdering a 14-year-old boy to sell him to a surgeon. Bishop admitted to stealing between 500 and 1,000 corpses and of murdering 3 people to sell their bodies. He was found guilty and hanged and dissected.

Burke and Hare

Some of the finest teaching hospitals of the period were in Edinburgh in Scotland. Surgeons would travel from as far away as North America to learn their trade at the Scottish hospitals. This popularity meant a large number of bodies were required for the students to practice on. William Burke and William Hare were happy to help.

This painting is from the inn near Edinburgh where Burke and Hare were said to drink.

William Hare and his wife owned a lodging house. One of their tenants died suddenly and left them with a large debt. Hare and his friend Burke took the tenant's body to the university to see if they could sell it. Dr. Knox, a renowned medical **lecturer**, paid a

good deal of money for the body, no questions asked. Burke and Hare decided to sell some more bodies. Instead of grave robbing which the painting above mistakenly shows, they actually simply murdered their victims. They are known to have killed 16 people, and possibly as many as 30. They targeted travelers or homeless people who would not be missed. They lured them into the lodging house and plied them with drink. Then they took them upstairs and suffocated them, which left no trace of murder on the body.

Dr. Robert Knox (left) was called "Old Cyclops" as he only had one eye.

Over time Burke and Hare became reckless and murdered several well-known people including a children's entertainer, "Daft Jamie." He was recognized by Dr. Knox's students, so to stop rumors Knox began to dissect the bodies face first.

Two of Hare's tenants became suspicious of their landlords' behavior, particularly their instructions to avoid the spare bedroom. They discovered the body of Mary Docherty under the bed and called the police. Burke and Hare were arrested. The police had little evidence of murder, due to their suffocation technique. They struck a deal with Hare that if he gave evidence against Burke, he and his wife would go free. Burke was convicted, and Hare escaped to Ireland. Burke was hanged and his body was donated to medical science. Today, his bones are still on display at the University of Edinburgh.

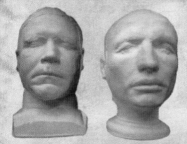

Burke's death mask (left) and a cast from life of Hare (right)

WHAT'S A BODY WORTH?

Burke and Hare saw that selling corpses was a way to earn good money. Children's bodies were sold by the inch. A child's body would fetch 6 shillings ($1.14) for the first foot, and nine pence (14 cents) per inch after that. Collectors paid greater sums for medical curiosities. In the 1780s, the anatomist John Hunter paid the enormous sum of £500 ($792) for the corpse of the "Irish Giant," whose huge skeleton is still displayed in the Royal College of Surgeons' Museum in London.

Presidents and Corpses

In North America, Philadelphia, Baltimore, and New York were well known for body snatching. Even presidents and their families became involved, either unwittingly as victims or by sharing a house with an anatomist involved with the trade.

Benjamin Franklin was one of the Founding Fathers of the United States. He was a leading author, printer, politician, postmaster, scientist, musician, inventor, and statesman. He lived for a few years in London, England, at 36 Craven Street, now a Benjamin Franklin museum. When recent restoration work was done on the house, a small pit was found in the basement room. About 1,200 pieces of human bone were recovered from the pit! The bones showed signs of dissection and medical experiments. An anatomy school had been run at the house by Benjamin Franklin's young friend, William Hewson. His subjects may have been stolen from nearby graveyards or have come from the weekly public executions at the gallows on the other side of the garden wall. Hewson died young of blood poisoning after he cut himself during a dissection.

A portrait of Benjamin Franklin during his time in London

THE PRESIDENT'S SON, AND FATHER!

John Scott Harrison (left) was the son of President William Henry Harrison and the father of President Benjamin Harrison. When he died in Ohio in 1878, his grave was protected by a brick vault, big stones mixed with the earth, and a watchman who checked the grave every hour for a week. The body of young Augustus Devin, buried the week before in the next grave, had been stolen. John Harrison's son and a friend of Devin's traveled to Cincinnati to look for Devin's body. They searched the Ohio Medical College. They discovered the body of John Harrison instead, hanging from a rope down a chute beneath a trapdoor. Devin's body was later found preserved in a vat of brine at the medical college of the University of Michigan!

There were riots against many American medical schools. When the grave of 17-year-old farmer's daughter Bathsheba Smith was robbed, people pointed angry fingers at nearby Yale Medical College. The next morning, a search of the medical school found nothing. As the search party was about to stop, they saw an area of floor had been recently disturbed, and under a large flat stone they discovered Bathsheba's body.

That night, a mob of about six hundred armed men hurled stones and burning coal at the medical building. Those responsible for the body snatching were never caught, but the riot continued for two nights!

REALLY?

Hiding places were quite sophisticated at some medical schools. They would store corpses inside domed roofs or used pulleys to hoist bodies into the chimneys of large fireplaces.

Body-Snatching World

The first known case of body snatching was committed by four medical students in Bologna, Italy, in 1319. There have been cases of body snatching in many countries around the world.

In Montreal, Canada, in 1875, typhoid fever struck a convent school. The dead children's corpses were taken by body snatchers before the children's relatives arrived to collect them. The Anatomy Act of Quebec was amended to prevent anything similar happening again. After the amendment, bodies still had to be claimed by a relative, however. If friends of the deceased tried to give them a decent burial, the body could still be given up for dissection. This happened to a sailor who fell overboard in the harbor at Montreal, to the annoyance of his friends.

In 1530s France, Flemish student Andreas Vesalius frequently robbed the Paris graveyards with fellow anatomy pupils. Body snatchers in France were called "les corbeaux" which means "the crows." Body snatching only resulted in a year's imprisonment and a fine.

Because the crime was a little easier to get away with in France and also in Ireland, bodies would sometimes be shipped to nearby England or Scotland in barrels or crates of brine or brandy!

In Dublin, Ireland, the medical schools during the 1700s and 1800s were on a constant hunt for bodies. Bullys' Acre was a burial ground with low walls and a lonely location. Soldiers at the nearby Royal Hospital would guard the graveyard. In November 1825, a sentry captured Thomas Tuite, a known resurrectionist, with five bodies and pockets full of teeth! To avoid being caught, gangs put leather shoes on the horse's hooves to muffle any noise. Sometimes they would dress the corpse in an old coat, and hold them up so that the corpse looked like a drunk being carried home.

WALKING DEAD

Margorie McCall from Lurgan, Ireland, got a fever and died in 1705. She was buried quickly to stop the disease from spreading. Resurrectionists dug her up a few hours later, and to steal her wedding ring one of them cut off her finger. To his horror Margorie woke up! She walked home, still dressed in her shroud, to her grieving family.

REALLY?

A **pathologist** in Dublin was caught body snatching with his students by a night watchman at Bullys' Acre. The watchman grabbed him by the legs. The students then pulled him by the arms. The students won the tug-of-war, but he died of his injuries shortly afterward!

Discrimination

Graveyards used to bury the poor or unclaimed were the easiest graveyards to body snatch from. They were unguarded and people generally turned a blind eye. Although records show that people of any race, sex, or social status were victims, the era of body snatching was a time of racial and social inequality in Europe and North America. This meant that immigrants, blacks, and the poor were most often targeted.

In Britain after the 1832 Anatomy Act, the corpses of any unclaimed dead could be given to anatomy schools. Because of this, hospitals were considered death houses, and only the most desperately ill people dared go to them. People were also afraid of dying in workhouses in case their bodies were sold for dissection. A workhouse was a place where those unable to support themselves were offered accommodation and employment. Life in a workhouse was hard, so only the truly desperate would want to go there. The Anatomy Act helped stop the crime of body snatching, but in reality it also legalized the use of poor people's corpses. Grave robbers were out of a job but a new breed of body snatchers were the officials and mortuary attendants.

Boys at an English workhouse around 1896

Potter's fields were graveyards for the unclaimed and poor. Many were divided into different areas for those who were or were not considered worthy of respect. There was a separate blacks' burying ground. Free blacks as well as slaves were buried there. Chris Baker was black and watched over the potter's field in the state of Virginia. He didn't protect the graves, though, he was a body snatcher for the Medical College of Virginia! He would often mourn at the funerals and then go back to snatch the bodies. When he snatched Clay Lomax's body, he had acted as pallbearer at the funeral.

REALLY?

The November 14th 1837 edition of the *Charlestown Courier* contained an advertisement that said: "Wanted fifty negroes. Any person having sick negroes, considered incurable by their respective physicians, and wishing to dispose of them, Dr. S. will pay cash."

STANDING UP TO INJUSTICE

In Philadelphia, Pennsylvania, in December 1882, it was discovered that six bodies had been dug up from Lebanon Cemetery, a black burial ground. The bodies were being taken to Jefferson Medical College for dissection. The African-American community was outraged, and a crowd gathered at the **morgue**. The crowd swore to get revenge on those who participated in digging up the graves. One man screamed when he found the body of his 29-year-old brother, and an elderly woman found her husband's body, whose burial she had only been able to afford by begging at the wharves where he had worked. Physician William S. Forbes was accused, and the case led to a new Anatomy Act being passed.

Mortsafes and Towers

At the beginning of the 1800s, there was a battle of wits between body snatchers and grieving relatives. Those who could afford it tried to ensure that their loved one's corpse would remain undisturbed. There was a widely held belief that there was a link between the fate of the corpse and the fate of the soul. **Dismemberment** was believed to deny a person **resurrection**.

One invention was the "coffin collar," a stout iron necklace bolted to the floor of the coffin to keep the body from being dragged out.

Heavy slabs of stone known as mort-stones were placed on top of the grave to deter the diggers. Once the body had rotted, the stone was removed until the next burial.

A mortsafe was an iron cage placed over the coffin in the grave and buried. It would be dug up again to be reused.

An alternative design was a cast-iron coffin-shaped box which was placed over the coffin and buried. Again, these iron coffin covers were eventually dug up for reuse.

mort-stone

mortsafe

coffin cover

People began to organize armed men to stand guard in graveyards at night. Watch houses were built, often a circular tower with the upper floor equipped with a fireplace and a window. A hole in the wall or window frame would allow the guards to shoot at anyone suspicious. There was usually a bell to raise the alarm and to seek assistance.

watch house

Mort-houses were solidly-built windowless vaults, with massive walls and heavy wooden and metal doors. Bodies were stored in these buildings until they had **decomposed** and were then buried in the usual way.

mort-house

GRAVE PROTECTION ON A BUDGET

The most basic method to make it harder for a body to be dug up was to pack the grave with bundles of straw, sticks, and large slabs of stone to slow down potential diggers. A more sophisticated variation was to place thick planks lengthwise across the coffin, forcing resurrectionists to dig up the entire grave. Poorer families would sometimes simply leave items like a stone or a blade of grass on the grave. If it had moved, they would know the grave had been tampered with. Some would fit iron straps and locks around wooden coffins. People also asked for their loved ones to be buried extra-deep, in the hope that if a body snatcher did dig that deep the hole's sides would cave in and bury them.

23

Is Archaeology Robbing?

If the definition of a robber is someone who takes items without their owners' permission, then archaeologists could be described as tomb robbers and body snatchers. The distinction lies in the intentions behind taking a body from its grave.

If you dig up an old coffin with the intention to steal a watch or a ring, that is called grave robbing, and it's illegal. If the site was a Native American burial plot and a university researcher applied for a permit to excavate the site, then it's archaeology, which is allowed by law. An archaeologist's job is to piece together human history and prehistory. Information is often gained by excavating tombs and burial grounds because humans have a long history of burying items important to the deceased with the body.

Grave robbers, on the other hand, sell found artifacts for profit to dishonest collectors. They have no interest in the historical significance of the object, just how much money it can fetch.

Archaeologists unearth human remains during a dig.

Mummies Snatched

High-status Egyptians were usually buried with valuable items to take with them to the afterlife. Egyptian priests around 1000 BCE wanted to move important mummies to a safe place away from grave robbers. Huge teams of local workers moved the heavy coffins and brought them in long processions down to the River Nile to be transported. They were moved to secret underground tombs to try to keep them safe from grave robbers. Many such hidden tombs have been found in the mountains near Thebes.

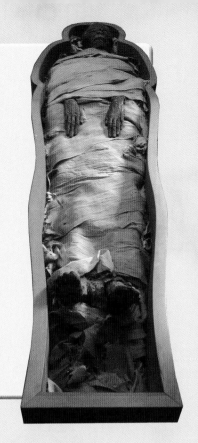

An Egyptian mummy kept in the Vatican Museums

In ancient Egypt, bodies were mummified in as lifelike a way as possible to provide a permanent home for the soul. Although the internal organs were removed during mummification, they were preserved in canopic jars and carefully kept with the rest of the body. In Victorian times, people didn't seem to worry that they were **desecrating** mummies by unwrapping them. Mummies exported to the United States were used in the papermaking industry or even, as Mark Twain reported, to be burned as railroad fuel!

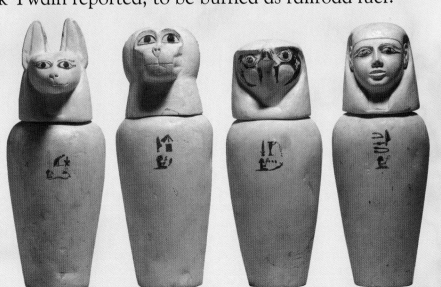

canopic jars

Booby Traps

When body-snatcher gangs sent pretend mourners to observe funerals, one of the things they were looking out for was booby traps. During the last years of the resurrection era, all sorts of machines were devised by families anxious to protect their dead.

The cemetery gun was usually a large smoothbore flintlock gun attached to a large block of wood. The block of wood was fixed to the ground with a couple of spikes. Trip wires around the grave would be connected to the gun's trigger. Loaded at night and left armed by the cemetery keeper, the device was more of a night watchman than anything else. The guns were disarmed during the day, and mourners and visitors knew better than to come back after dark. Many a crafty keeper would move his weapons around at sunset to surprise any body snatchers who had scouted the graveyard the previous day.

The cemetery gun could be loaded with rock salt or birdshot to scare away an intruder, or a heavier shot to maim or even kill.

GRAVE TORPEDO

Thomas N. Howell invented two different grave torpedoes. One was a little like a landmine. It weighed 8 pounds (3.62 kg) and carried a charge of black powder ignited by a percussion cap. Buried on top of the coffin, if the metal plate was disturbed, it would fire right at the would-be grave robber. An advertisement for the weapon said the deceased could "sleep well sweet angel, let no fears of ghouls disturb thy rest, for above thy shrouded form lies a torpedo, ready to make minced meat of anyone who attempts to convey you to the pickling vat."

In 1881, at least three innocent men were killed when one went off during a late night walk through the cemeteries near Gann in Knox County, Ohio!

One of Howell's torpedoes

Another invention was a shotgun that went off if the coffin lid was opened. Grave robbers had better beware when digging in some of these graveyards! Trip wires attached to the lid would pull the pin and the shot would be fired.

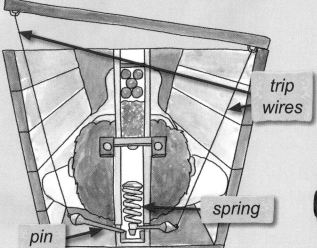

trip wires

spring

pin

REALLY?

There is one report of a father who filled his child's coffin with gunpowder and fused it so that it would explode if disturbed.

Modern Body Snatching

Body snatching still can occur today. The reasons why the bodies are stolen have changed, however. They can be stolen for a ransom or to cause distress to families. Bodies can also be used for medical science, organ donation, or for religious ritual. Bizarrely, they can also be used for marriage!

Funeral homes in New York, New Jersey, and Pennsylvania, and employees of a biomedical supply company were charged with body stealing and unlawful dissection in 2007. They secretly removed skin, bone, and other body parts from corpses awaiting cremation. The funeral-home owners made millions of dollars by selling the body parts. They took bones from the body of well-known TV host Alistair Cooke, who died in 2004. They replaced his bones with PVC pipe before his cremation. They sold the bones for bone grafts, but as the cancer that killed Cooke had spread to his bones, this was very unsafe. Reports indicated that his death certificate was altered to hide his cause of death and reduce his age from 95 to 85.

presenter and journalist
Alistair Cooke

In the United Kingdom, the remains of Gladys Hammond were stolen from a churchyard by animal rights extremists campaigning against a facility which bred guinea pigs for scientific research. Hammond was the mother-in-law of one of the farm's owners. Four leaders of the "Save the Newchurch Guinea Pigs" campaign group were jailed for conspiracy to blackmail. Hammond's remains were recovered.

In China there has been a resurgence in the old custom of "ghost marriages" in some coal-mining regions. Superstitious families pay high prices for female corpses to marry their deceased unmarried male relatives. The high death toll among young male miners has led to body snatchers stealing and then selling corpses to families. In 2007, a convicted grave robber was arrested for murdering six women and selling their bodies as "ghost brides."

VOODOO PARTS

Body parts are believed to have magical powers in some belief systems such as voodoo. Tomb raiders dug up more than 100 corpses at a cemetery in Benin, West Africa, in 2012. The body parts bring a premium price on the black market. At Lincoln Park Cemetery in Miami, Florida, the bodies of at least three deceased babies were missing from their graves. The bones of adults were also found scattered around. A dead chicken had been placed in one of the empty vaults, raising the suspicion that it was the work of people who practice voodoo or similar rituals.

Glossary

anatomy
A branch of knowledge that deals with the structure of organisms.

archaeologist
A person studying past human life as shown by fossil relics and the monuments and tools left by ancient peoples.

autopsy
An examination of a dead body to find out the cause of death.

decompose
To break down or rot through chemical change.

desecrating
Treating a sacred place or sacred object with great disrespect.

dismemberment
Cutting off or separating the limbs.

dissection
Cutting up into separate parts for examination and study.

lecturer
A person who teaches at a university.

libel
Something spoken, written, or drawn that injures a person's good name.

mirror-writing
Backward writing you can read in a mirror.

morgue
A place where the bodies of the dead are kept until they are identified or released for burial.

pathologist
An expert in the study of diseases.

resurrection
A belief in the rising again to life of human dead before the final judgment.

resurrectionist
One who steals bodies from graves in order to sell them for dissection.

shrouds
The cloths placed over or around a dead body.

For More Information
Books

MacDonald, Fiona. *You Wouldn't Want to Meet a Body Snatcher! Criminals and Murderers You'd Rather Avoid.* Franklin Watts, 2009.

Shultz, Suzanne. *Body Snatching: The Robbing of Graves for the Education of Physicians in Early Nineteenth Century America.* McFarland & Company, 2005.

Websites

Body Snatchers
www.encyclopedia.com/topic/body_snatching.aspx
Learn information about body snatchers from various encyclopedias.

Mortsafes
www.historyhouse.co.uk/articles/mortsafes.html
Read about the attempts to prevent the resurrection men from taking away dead bodies.

William Burke & William Hare, 'The Resurrectionists'
www.scotshistoryonline.co.uk/burke.html
Learn about Burke and Hare, the infamous Scottish body snatchers.

Index